discover countries

Italy

Kelly Davis

WAYLAND

First published in 2012 by Wayland
Copyright Wayland 2012

Wayland
Hachette Children's Books
338 Euston Road
London NW1 3BH

Wayland Australia
Level 17/207 Kent Street,
Sydney, NSW 2000

Concept design: Jason Billin
Editors: Victoria Brooker and Kelly Davis
Design: 320 Design Ltd
Consultants: Paola Argiroffi Woolf and Elaine Jackson

Produced for Wayland by
White-Thomson Publishing Ltd

www.wtpub.co.uk
+44 (0)843 2087 460

British Library Cataloguing in Publication Data

Davis, Kelly.
Italy. -- (Discover countries)
1. Italy -- Juvenile literature.
I. Title II. Series
945'.09312-dc23

ISBN-13: 978 0 7502 6934 6
Printed in China

Wayland is a division of Hachette Children's Books
an Hachette UK company
www.hachette.co.uk

All data in this book was researched in 2011
and has been collected from the latest sources available at that time.

Picture credits
1, Dreamstime/Morozena; 4 (map), Stefan Chabluk; 5, Dreamstime/Honjune; 6,Dreamstime/Ralukatudor; 7, Dreamstime/Vulkanette;
8, SteveWhite-Thomson; 9, Alamy/Cipriansalceanu; 10, Dreamstime/Maudanros; 11, Shutterstock/Danilo Ascione; 12, Dreamstime/Valeria73;
13, Alamy/Arif Iqball; 14, Steve White-Thomson; 15, Shutterstock/Selfiy; 16, Steve White-Thomson; 17, Dreamstime/Maudanros;
18, Dreamstime/Littleny; 19, Shutterstock/Giuseppe Fucile; 20, Shutterstock/Neil Roy Johnson; 21, Dreamstime/Bobsphotography;
22 Steve White-Thomson; 23, Dreamstime/Draghicich; 24, Dreamstime/Morozena; 25, Shutterstock/Pinosub; 26, Dreamstime/Diliff;
27, Dreamstime/Ratmandude; 28, Dreamstime/Franckgrondin; 29, Shutterstock/Ziga Camernik;
cover (right) Shutterstock/Michaela Stejskalova; cover (left) Dreamstime/Bobsphotography.

Contents

Discovering Italy

Italy is shaped like a high-heeled boot, sticking out from the European mainland into the Mediterranean Sea, 'kicking' the island of Sicily. The island of Sardinia, to the west, is part of Italy too, along with about 70 other, smaller islands. There are also two tiny, self-governing states within the Italian mainland – San Marino and the Vatican City.

Land of mountains and vineyards

Northernmost Italy is bordered by the snowy peaks of the Italian Alps. Below the mountains lies the rich farmland of the North Italian Plain, as well as the wealthy 'industrial triangle' containing the cities of Milan, Genoa and Turin. Southern Italy is much poorer and more rural than the north. The south of the country mainly depends on tourism and growing grapes (for wine) and olives (for olive oil).

A dramatic history

The mighty Roman Empire began in Rome over 2,000 years ago. At its height, the empire stretched from Scotland in the north to the African deserts in the south.

Italy is a little larger than the United Kingdom. This map shows Italy's main cities, regions, bordering countries and its two biggest islands.

DID YOU KNOW?

The ancient Romans spoke Latin, which became the basis of many European languages, such as Italian, Spanish, Portugese, French and English.

From 1922 to 1943, the Fascist Party (led by Benito Mussolini) ruled Italy under a very harsh, extreme, nationalist system. In 1939, Mussolini signed an agreement with Adolf Hitler, the German leader. Italy then entered World War II in 1940 as a German ally. It became a republic in 1946 and was one of the first members of the European Union (EU) in 1951.

Italy today

Although Italy remains a popular tourist destination, it faces some major challenges, especially its huge public debt – nearly 2 trillion euros in 2011. Many of its political and business leaders have faced charges of corruption, and the country was affected by the 2008 global financial crisis. The former prime minister, Silvio Berlusconi, was accused of financial and moral wrongdoing. In November 2011, he finally stepped down after 17 years, and was replaced by Mario Monti.

Italy statistics

Area: 301,340 sq km (116,348 sq miles)

Capital city: Rome

Government type: Republic

Bordering countries/states: Austria, France, Vatican City, San Marino, Switzerland

Currency: Euro

Language: Italian (official), German (parts of Trentino-Alto Adige region are predominantly German speaking), French (small French-speaking minority in Valle d'Aosta region), Slovene (Slovene-speaking minority in the Trieste-Gorizia area)

◀ Visitors sit on the Spanish Steps, the widest staircase in Europe and a popular tourist attraction in Rome.

Landscape and climate

Much of Italy has a Mediterranean climate, with hot, dry summers and wet, cool winters. Temperature differences between different parts of the country are more dramatic in winter. In the Italian Alps, in the far north, temperatures go below freezing in winter but can rise as high as 30° Celsius in the summer. There are also frequent thunderstorms, especially in northern areas.

Basking on the beach

With its long, jagged coastline, full of little bays and inlets, Italy has many popular beach resorts. These coastal areas usually get much warmer weather than the mountainous regions in the centre of the country.

▼ The narrow strip of land next to the Ligurian Sea, near Genoa, is known as the Italian Riviera.

Wet plains and mountain ranges

The North Italian Plain gets a lot of rain. This rich farming land also benefits from the waters of the River Po, which flows eastward to the Adriatic Sea.

Mountain ranges cover more than a third of Italy, and attract climbers and skiers from all over the world. The Alps and the Dolomites are located in the north, while the Appenines form a spine running down the central length of the country. The rest of Italy is largely covered by rolling hills.

Volcanoes and earthquakes

Environmental hazards, including landslides, avalanches, flooding and earthquakes, cause a lot of problems. In 2009, an earthquake in Abruzzo (in central Italy) killed more than 200 people and left thousands homeless.

Italy also has several volcanoes. Mount Etna, on the island of Sicily, is Europe's most active volcano and threatens nearby villages. Mount Vesuvius, which destroyed the Roman city of Pompeii in 79 CE, could erupt again. Millions of people still live near it, in the Bay of Naples, despite the danger.

▶ The volcano Stromboli (on the island of the same name) regularly spews out red-hot lava. It has become known as 'the Lighthouse of the Mediterranean'.

Facts at a glance

Land area: 294,140 sq km (113,568 sq miles)

Highest point: Mont Blanc (Monte Bianco) de Courmayeur 4,748 m (15,577 ft)

Longest river: Po 645 km (400 miles)

Coastline: 7,600 km (4,722 miles)

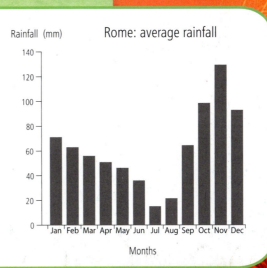

Temperature (°C) — Rome: average temperature — Months

Rainfall (mm) — Rome: average rainfall — Months

Population and health

Italy's varied population has been shaped by its history. In the 18th and 19th centuries, parts of the country were invaded by Austrian and Spanish forces. Later, Italy gained some African colonies (including Eritrea and Ethiopia), and occupied Albania during World War II. These events explain why many Italians have ancestors who came from other countries.

A shrinking population

A lot of Italians emigrated in the past, particularly to South America and the USA. But Italy had a high birth rate so the population stayed about the same size. In the 1970s, the birth rate began to fall. Since then, there have been concerns that there are too many pensioners taking money out of the economy (in the form of pensions), and not enough younger, working people putting money into the economy. Between 2010 and 2011, the population started to rise very slightly, by 0.42 per cent. However, this rise seems to be entirely due to immigration.

Facts at a glance

Total population: 61 million
Life expectancy at birth: 81.8 years
Children dying before 5th birthday: 0.4%
Ethnic composition: Italian (includes small clusters of German-, French-, and Slovene-Italians in the north and Albanian-Italians and Greek-Italians in the south)

DID YOU KNOW?
Trentino-Alto Adige, in northern Italy, is partly German-speaking, and there is a small French-speaking group in Valle d'Aosta, in the Italian Alps.

◀ Nearly 22 per cent of the Italian population will be over 65 by 2015. This will place a big burden on the Italian economy.

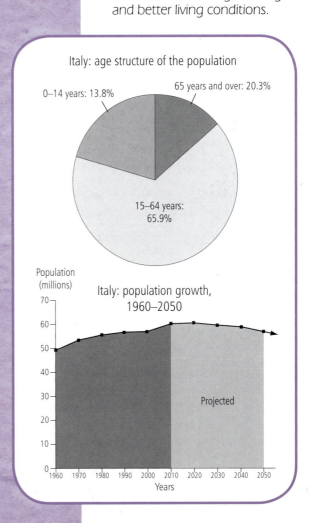

North African immigrants march in Rome, demanding more rights and better living conditions.

Increasing immigration

In the late 20th century, immigrants from North Africa, Eastern Europe, South America and South-East Asia came to Italy, and helped reverse the effects of the falling birth rate. Since the series of revolutions that began in late 2010 (known as 'the Arab Spring'), many North Africans (especially Tunisians and Libyans) have been arriving.

Health in Italy

As Italy has a large elderly population, some of whom have health problems, the government has to spend around 9 per cent of its Gross Domestic Product (GDP) on healthcare. However, most people enjoy good health and a life expectancy that is among the highest in Europe. Alcohol-related disease used to be a major problem in the 1970s, but Italians have since halved the average amount of alcohol they drink.

Italy: age structure of the population

0–14 years: 13.8%

65 years and over: 20.3%

15–64 years: 65.9%

Population (millions)

Italy: population growth, 1960–2050

Projected

Years

Settlements and living

Just over two-thirds of Italians live in urban settlements, mainly in the north of the country, in bustling cities such as Milan and Turin. This part of Italy offers more employment, mostly in manufacturing and service industries. The remaining third of the population live in villages, in the rural south and on Italy's many islands, where most of the jobs are in farming and tourism.

Regions and hill towns

Italy is divided into 20 regions (see map, p. 4), and each region has its own capital. For example, Bologna is the capital city of Emilia-Romagna. Every region also has numerous hill towns, and Tuscany and Umbria are particularly famous for these small settlements. Almost all Italy's hill towns were built in the medieval period, often to protect trade routes. They usually have a castle in the centre, and the town is surrounded by cliffs, thick stone walls or steep banks, which made it easier to defend hundreds of years ago.

Facts at a glance

Urban population: 68.4% (41.7 million)

Rural population: 31.6% (19.3 million)

Population of largest city: Rome 3.4 million

DID YOU KNOW?

In 2011, the village of Filettino (population 550), near Rome, declared its independence from Italy. The villagers even have their own currency, the 'Fiorito'.

Castelvecchio di Rocca Barbena, in Liguria, is a typical hill town. The name 'Castelvecchio' means 'Old Castle'.

Living close together

Most urban residents live in apartment buildings, as they can house a lot of people in a small space very efficiently. However, there have been problems with some builders not following official building regulations and using poor-quality materials. In a few cases, apartment blocks have even collapsed.

A meeting place

All Italian settlements, whether large or small, have at least one central piazza (square), where people walk, talk, sit in cafés or bars and celebrate festivals. The piazza is often in front of a church, usually paved and may have a central fountain or statue. Many piazzas have a busy market, selling fresh fruit and vegetables.

⬯ Like many Italian apartment blocks, this building in Sorrento, southern Italy, has blinds to block out the bright sunlight, and balconies for residents to sit outside.

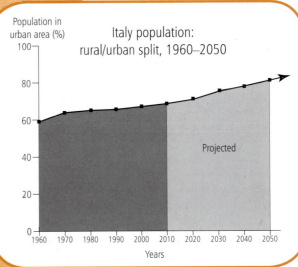

Population in urban area (%)

Italy population: rural/urban split, 1960–2050

Projected

Years

Family life

Italy has a strong tradition of family life, with family members often gathering for meals. Several generations sometimes share the same house or apartment building, or live very near each other. Many small Italian businesses are also run by members of a single family, who work together.

Smaller families

However, since the early 1970s, there have been some big changes in Italian family life, especially the fact that Italian women have been having fewer children. Some people blame the lack of flexible working arrangements for the falling birth rate, as it is difficult for women to combine full-time work with motherhood.

Facts at a glance

Average children per childbearing woman:
1.4 children

Average household size:
2.4 people

▼ Parents and children (and a few pets) take part in the annual Family Run in Vigevano, northern Italy.

Young Italians have also been taking longer to finish their education, leave home and get married. In fact, more than 60 per cent of young unmarried Italians aged below 34 live with their parents (the highest percentage in Europe). High youth unemployment makes it difficult for young people to afford their own homes.

A Venetian bride releases a pigeon. Doves used to be released at Italian weddings, as a sign of love and happiness, but they are now usually replaced by pigeons.

Fewer marriages and more divorces

Fewer Italians have been getting married, and between 2009 and 2010 the number of marriages went down slightly. Divorce used to be illegal in Italy, and the Catholic Church still disapproves of it. But, since it became legal in the 1970s, the divorce rate has been rising steadily.

Looking after the elderly

Italian families used to care for their elderly relatives themselves, and they are often very reluctant to put them in nursing homes. For this reason, many Italians now pay immigrants to care for their elderly family members in their own homes.

DID YOU KNOW?

At an Italian wedding, the bride and groom break a glass. The number of shattered pieces represent the number of happy years the couple will share together.

Religion and beliefs

Most Italians are Catholic and go to church services at Christmas and Easter. Only about one-third of Italian Catholics go to church regularly on Sundays. But some older people, especially in rural areas, go every day. Most of the Catholic religious festivals in Italy celebrate the Madonna (the mother of Jesus) or various saints. Church congregations are generally shrinking.

The Roman Catholic Church

The worldwide Roman Catholic Church is led by the pope, who lives in the Vatican Palace. Since 1929, the Vatican City has been recognised by Italy as an independent state, with its own small army and police force. Many Catholic religious orders started in Italy. These include the Franciscans, founded by St Francis, who came from Assisi, in Umbria.

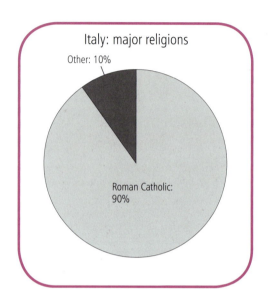

Italy: major religions

Other: 10%

Roman Catholic: 90%

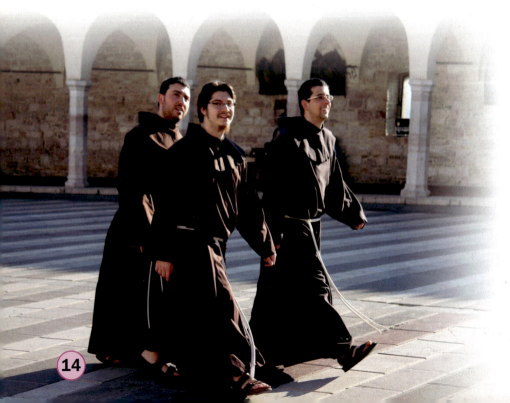

◀ Young Franciscan friars (monks who work in the community), follow the example of St Francis of Assisi by caring for the poor.

Protestants and Muslims

There is also a small Protestant community in Italy. This is made up of Baptists, Methodists, Lutherans and members of other Protestant churches.

Italy's Muslim population is growing because of immigration from Morocco, North Africa, South Asia, the Middle East and Albania. There are now more than a million Muslims living in Italy, and cultural differences have caused some tensions. For example, in August 2011, the government was considering passing a law banning Muslim women from covering their faces with veils.

Italian Jews

Jewish communities have existed in Italy for centuries, although an estimated 7,500 Italian Jews were killed by the Germans in World War II. There are still around 45,000 Jews in Italy, many of them living in Rome and Turin.

🔺 Pope Benedict XVI blesses people in St Peter's Square, outside the Vatican Palace. Every year, thousands of Catholics visit the Vatican City, hoping to see the pope.

Education and learning

Italian school students generally achieve just below the average for developed countries. But students in northern Italy usually gain much better grades than those in the south, mainly because of poorer-quality teaching in the south. One possible reason for this difference is that politicians in the south are said to reward their supporters by giving them teaching jobs, whether or not they are properly qualified.

🔻 Teenagers enjoy going on a school outing in Bologna, in northern Italy.

The Italian school system

Italy has both private and state education systems. State education is compulsory from the age of 6 to 16. Kindergarten (for children up to about 3) and infant school (for children aged 3 to 6) are both optional. Between 6 and 11, all pupils must attend primary school. Then they go to lower secondary school, from the age of 11 to 14.

There are two types of upper secondary school, which pupils attend from around 14 to 19: the *liceo* and the *istituto*. Most school districts have *licei* specialising in classics, science and art; and *istituti* offering technical, vocational and teacher training courses.

Italian universities

Italian students are usually 19 or 20 by the time they go to university. Most degree courses used to last four or five years – and sometimes took even longer to complete. Now there are some three-year degree courses available but some employers still prefer to take on five-year graduates.

Challenges in universities

Italian universities have suffered from many problems, particularly corruption and nepotism amongst staff, which have led to low teaching standards. The government started reforming the university system in 2010. The changes led to funding cuts of at least 300 million euros in 2011, causing widespread student protests.

Italy spends less than 5 per cent of its GDP on education. In 2010, thousands of students protested against cuts in government spending on universities.

DID YOU KNOW?
The University of Bologna, which was founded in 1088, is thought to be the oldest university in the Western world.

Employment and economy

Italy's mainly industrial and service-based economy is the third-biggest in the eurozone. The north has a lot of manufacturing companies, while the south depends more on agriculture and tourism. Economically, the north and south are very deeply divided. The annual GDP per capita (per person) in the north is 30,000 euros, while the average in the south is around 16,000 euros.

Keeping it in the family

Many Italian shops and restaurants are run and staffed by members of a single family. Small and medium-sized family businesses also produce many of the stylish leather goods and delicious food products that Italy is known for.

Facts at a glance

Economic structure:
agriculture: 1.9%
industry: 25.3%
services: 72.8%

Labour force:
agriculture: 4.2%
industry: 30.7%
services: 65.1%
Female labour force: 40% of total
Unemployment rate: 8.4%

▼ Italy has over 4 million businesses employing fewer than ten people, like these shops and restaurants.

▶ Thousands of people in Rome protested against government cuts, in 2011.

These small, family-run companies, which make up about 95 per cent of Italian enterprises, have been particularly badly affected by the recession, triggered by the 2008 global financial crisis.

Economic challenges

Italy's main economic weaknesses are: relatively high wages, lack of investment, the country's ageing population, and non-payment of taxes because of the large 'black market' economy. 'Black market' employment (in which workers are paid in cash and don't pay tax) is most common in agriculture, building and service industries, and accounts for around 27 per cent of Italy's GDP. Unemployment is also a major problem, though it is much worse in the south than the north.

Italy's debt mountain

At present, economists are particularly worried about Italy's huge public debt. In 2011, this reached nearly 2 trillion euros (or 120 per cent of Italy's national output). Because its economy is growing so slowly, Italy now has to pay a very high rate of interest on money that it borrows (while France and Germany pay much less). All this has been causing a lot of anxiety in the EU – because the funds set aside by the EU for emergencies would not be big enough to rescue an economy the size of Italy's.

DID YOU KNOW?

In 2011, Italian youth (aged 15 to 24) had an unemployment rate of around 30 per cent, one of the highest in the developed world.

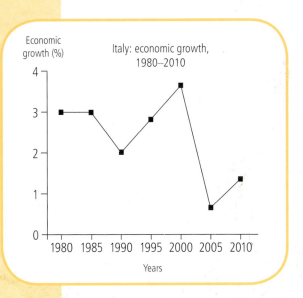
Italy: economic growth, 1980–2010

Industry and trade

The biggest Italian industries are motor vehicles, textiles, clothing, footwear, pottery, tourism, machinery, iron and steel, chemicals and food processing. But most Italian manufacturers are relatively small enterprises.

Fast cars and high fashion

Italy is best known for high-quality, luxury brands. In the Italian car industry, some of the biggest names are Fiat, Ferrari, Alfa Romeo, Lamborghini and Maserati, which are all prized for their speed, comfort and stylish design. Meanwhile, in the world of fashion, Italian designer brands, such as Armani, Prada and Gucci, are frequently worn by film stars and other celebrities.

DID YOU KNOW? Michele Ferrero (Italy's own Willy Wonka') has a company, with 18 factories worldwide, that makes Nutella, Kinder snacks and Tic Tacs.

This red Ferrari is one of the world's most desirable cars.

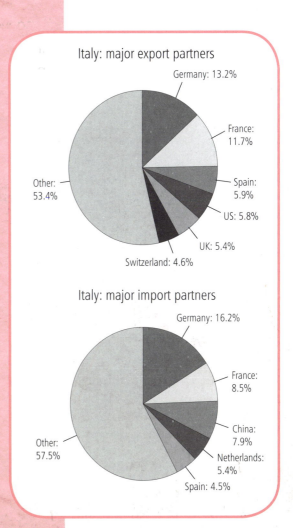

A model on the catwalk at a Milan fashion show. Milan is one of the four fashion capitals of the world, alongside London, Paris and New York.

Natural resources

Italy's natural resources include coal, mercury, zinc, pumice and marble. The white marble quarried in Tuscany has been used in sculptures and buildings worldwide. Italy has some natural gas and crude oil of its own but imports most of its supply.

Selling goods abroad

Italy mainly exports electronic products, textiles and clothing, machinery, motor vehicles, chemicals, food, tobacco, minerals and metals. It leads the world in olive oil production, and is a major exporter of rice, tomatoes and wine.

The 2008 recession reduced Italy's exports – from US$546.9 billion in 2008 to US$369 billion in 2010. Since 2001, Italy's trade (especially in textiles) has suffered greatly from Chinese competition. Italian textiles used to make up around 18 per cent of the country's exports, but this figure has now shrunk to about 11 per cent.

Italy: major export partners
- Germany: 13.2%
- France: 11.7%
- Spain: 5.9%
- US: 5.8%
- UK: 5.4%
- Switzerland: 4.6%
- Other: 53.4%

Italy: major import partners
- Germany: 16.2%
- France: 8.5%
- China: 7.9%
- Netherlands: 5.4%
- Spain: 4.5%
- Other: 57.5%

Farming and food

Although Italian farm produce (especially cheese, grapes and olives) is prized all over the world, agriculture provided only 1.9 per cent of the country's GDP in 2010. The warm Mediterranean climate helps farmers produce a variety of crops, but the mountainous landscape makes farming difficult in much of Italy. Having a long coastline, the country has a rich harvest of fish.

Help from the EU

With its wet climate and rich soil, the North Italian Plain is suited to large-scale grain and rice production. This type of farming is profitable – because of funding from the EU Common Agricultural Policy (CAP) and because it is well organised. Farmers have formed co-operatives, which make production and distribution cheaper.

Many different types of smoked ham and salami are made from the pork produced by Italian pig farmers.

During the 1980s, the CAP provided money to modernise Italian farming through increased use of machinery. It also encouraged farmers to combine their land, creating larger farms.

Farming in southern Italy

Farmers in the south tend to own smaller farms, and specialise in growing fruit (such as oranges and lemons from Sicily), as well as olives, wine and tomatoes. The hot, dry climate and poorer soil make farming more difficult and less profitable here.

Pasta and pizza

Pasta is one of the best-known Italian dishes. It was probably introduced to Sicily by Arab invaders in the 8th century. There are around 350 different varieties of dried pasta, ranging from *farfalle* (resembling bows) to *racchette* (shaped like tennis rackets).

Pizza is another Italian food that is eaten all over the world. Some say it dates back to flatbreads eaten by the ancient Greeks and Romans, and others claim it was invented by ancient Persians or Egyptians. However, we do know that modern pizza was first made in Naples in the early 19th century.

▶ Ingredients for a typical Italian meal (olive oil, spaghetti, garlic, mushrooms, tomatoes and fresh basil), and the ever-popular pizza.

DID YOU KNOW?

Pasta nera is flavoured with squid or cuttlefish ink, which turns it black! This type of pasta is often served with a shellfish sauce.

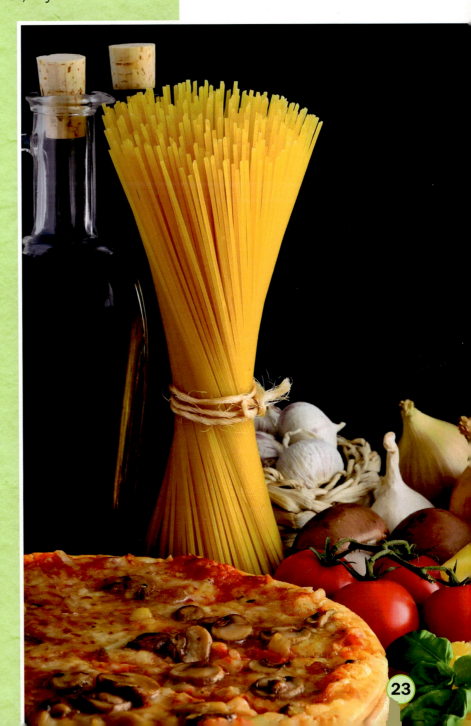

Transport and communications

Italy has a good transport network – by road, rail, air and water. Telecommunications are also very up to date, with just over half the population having access to the Internet in 2010. There are about 6,700 km (4,160 miles) of motorways in Italy in total. Most of them are well maintained and road users pay for them by means of a toll system.

Ferries and gondolas

As Italy has around 70 small islands, as well as the large islands of Sicily and Sardinia, ferries are needed to transport people and goods to and from the mainland.

> **Facts at a glance**
>
> **Total roads:** 487,700 km (303,043 miles)
>
> **Paved roads:** 487,700 km (303,043 miles)
>
> **Railways:** 20,254 km (12,585 miles)
>
> **Major airports:** 30
>
> **Major ports:** Augusta, Cagliari, Genoa, Livorno, Taranto, Trieste, Venice

▼ A gondola (in the foreground) and a water bus on the Grand Canal, which snakes through the centre of Venice.

Some of the main northern ferry terminals include Genoa and Livorno; while Naples and Salerno operate ferries in the southwest. Travellers going to Greece will catch a ferry from Brindisi in the southeast. Italians make use of water to travel within cities as well as between islands. Venice is famous for its canals, which serve the same purpose as roads in the old city centre.

Planes and trains

As one of the world's top tourist destinations, Italy has plenty of modern, well-equipped airports to handle the many thousands of travellers arriving there every day. The two main international airports are in Rome and Milan, with direct connections to European and North American cities.

The trains are relatively inexpensive and there is an excellent rail system throughout the country. One of the most picturesque Italian railways is the *Trenino Verde* ('Little Green Train') in Sardinia, which runs for 160 km (100 miles). Passengers can enjoy views of green valleys and vineyards, and dramatic rock faces, as they travel across the island.

○ The Alta Velocità, a high-speed Italian train, can travel from Rome to Milan in 3.5 hours.

DID YOU KNOW?
From the age of 14, Italian teenagers are legally permitted to ride mopeds, which can travel at a maximum speed of 50 kmh (30 mph).

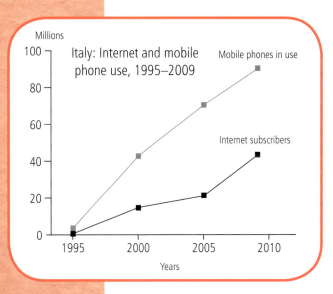

Millions

Italy: Internet and mobile phone use, 1995–2009

Mobile phones in use

Internet subscribers

100
80
60
40
20
0

1995   2000   2005   2010

Years

Leisure and tourism

Every year, millions of tourists visit historic cities such as Rome, Florence, Siena and Pisa. Including jobs indirectly supported by the tourist industry, tourism provides nearly 10 per cent of employment in Italy.

Art and architecture

A lot of tourists come to Italy to see paintings, sculptures and buildings (such as the Leaning Tower of Pisa). Many of these artworks date from the early 1400s to around 1600, a period known as the Renaissance. During this time, Italian artists were very influenced by ancient Greek and Roman art. Leonardo da Vinci painted the *Mona Lisa* and Michelangelo carved his statue *David*.

Facts at a glance

Tourist arrivals (millions)
Year	Arrivals
1995	31.1
2000	41.2
2005	36.5
2009	43.2

▼ The Colosseum, where chariot races were held more than 1,900 years ago, is now one of Rome's most popular tourist attractions.

Music and films

The first opera was performed in Florence around 1600. In the 19th and 20th centuries, composers such as Giuseppe Verdi and Giacomo Puccini wrote operas that influenced musicians in France, Germany and other countries. Later, in the 20th century, Italian film-makers like Federico Fellini and Luchino Visconti led the way for many British and American film directors.

Sporting victories

Today, many Italians still love going to the opera and the cinema. They also spend a lot of time watching and participating in sport. Football is extremely popular, and the Italian National Football team has won four FIFA World Cup titles – the last time in 2006.

Italian motorcyclist, Valentino Rossi, has won nine Grand Prix World Championships. Many Italians also love cycling. Every May, people compete in the Giro d'Italia, a long-distance cycling race, which lasts about three weeks. Other popular sports include volleyball, basketball and winter sports; and Italy has twice won Olympic gold for cross-country skiing.

Soccer fans, with their faces painted the colours of the Italian flag, support their team at the 2010 FIFA World Cup.

DID YOU KNOW?
The Ferrari F1 Motor Racing Team is the most successful Formula One team in history, having won 15 drivers' championship titles.

Environment and wildlife

Italy has many protected marine areas and nature reserves, including 24 national parks. The first national park to be established, in 1922, was Gran Paradiso (in northwestern Italy). This park includes deep valleys, high mountain peaks, rocky slopes, glaciers, lakes, marshes and Alpine pastures. This varied landscape supports a wide range of plants, such as larch and fir trees and Alpine flowers, as well as several rare animals and birds.

Endangered wildlife

There are many threats to Italian wildlife, including agriculture, hunting, poaching and forest fires. Coastal development has also caused problems. According to the World Wide Fund for Nature (WWF), the ever-increasing numbers of tourists visiting Italian beach resorts have led to excessive development and pollution on the Mediterranean coast, which has damaged marine life.

Facts at a glance

Proportion of area protected: 11.2%

Biodiversity (known species): 6,321

Threatened species: 9

▼ Gran Paradiso National Park covers about 70,000 hectares (173,000 acres) and includes many different habitats.

On the land, a number of animals are at risk of dying out. These vulnerable species include the Eurasian otter, the garden dormouse, six types of bat, the mouflon (a type of wild sheep), and wild goats. The Mediterranean monk seal is critically endangered, which means that there is an extremely high risk that it will die out.

Returning wildlife

However, in some remote areas agriculture has been abandoned, which has helped the wildlife recover. Italian woodlands have increased from 20 per cent to 30 per cent of the country's total surface area, and this has led to many conservation success stories. For example, in the Apennine mountains, red and roe deer and wild boar have returned, after being forced out over 100 years ago. Wolves, brown bears and bearded vultures have also started to return to their forest habitats.

▲ The European lynx returned to forested parts of the Italian Alps in the 1980s, after it had been reintroduced in neighbouring countries.

DID YOU KNOW?

In 2011, conservationists estimated that there were only around 600 Mediterranean monk seals left.

Glossary

ally country that agrees to co-operate with another country, especally in a war

avalanche when a large mass of snow or rock falls down a mountainside

birth rate number of births per 1,000 people, over a year

classics study of Latin and ancient Greek

colony country that is controlled by another country

compulsory something that must be done

congregation people who regularly worship at a church

conservation protection of wildlife and plants

corruption dishonesty, especially offering people money to do things that are against the law

earthquake sudden movement of the Earth's crust

economy way in which trade and money are controlled by a country

emigrate leave the country of one's birth

erupt burst or explode

eurozone group of EU countries that use the euro as their currency

export good or service that is sold to another country

Fascist Party political party, created by Benito Mussolini, which ruled Italy from 1922 to 1943

GDP total value of goods and services produced by a country

habitat place where a plant or animal usually lives

immigration people moving to a country that is not their place of birth

immigrant someone who moves to a country that is not their place of birth

import buy a good or service from another country

interest fee paid for the use of borrowed money

investment putting money into a business in order to make more money

lava hot, liquid rock that reaches the Earth's surface when a volcano erupts

life expectancy average period that a person may be expected to live

medieval from a historical period often dated from between about 476 and 1453 CE

nationalist very strongly loyal to one's own nation

nepotism when someone in a position of power favours close friends or relatives

opera drama in which singing takes the place of speech

poaching hunting illegally

private education education paid for by parents, rather than the government

public debt total amount owed by a country's government

recession period of significant decline in business activity

reform improve by changing

religious order group of monks, nuns or friars

Renaissance revival of ancient Greek and Roman art, architecture and learning, which started in 14th-century Italy

republic state that has a president rather than a king or queen

revolution when a government is overthrown

service industries businesses that provide services, such as sales, transport and banking

textile fabric or cloth

trillion 1,000 billion

urban in a town or city

vocational relating to a skill that is needed to carry out a trade

Topic web

Use this topic web to explore themes related to Italy
in different areas of your curriculum.

Maths
You are cooking pasta for lunch. You need to allow about 115 g (4 oz) dried pasta per person. How much pasta will you need for four?

Music
Watch some video clips, on YouTube, of Puccini's opera *Madame Butterfly*.

History
Using reference books, find out about the ancient Romans, their way of life, and how their empire grew and later ended.

English
What was the story of Shakespeare's play *The Merchant of Venice*? Find a summary on the Internet, watch the DVD or read the play.

Italy

Science
Why does Italy have so many volcanoes and earthquakes? See if you can answer this question by looking at reference books and the Internet.

Art
Look up Leonardo da Vinci's *Mona Lisa*, on Google Images and you will see many different versions of this famous painting. Try to sketch your own version.

Geography
Italy's best-known islands are Sardinia and Sicily. Find out about life on one of these islands.

ICT
Using the Internet, plan a two-week holiday in Italy, spending one week in the north and one week in the south. Make sure you spend some time in the mountains, some time on the beach and some time in a historic city.

Further information and index

Further reading

Countries in Our World: Italy by Ann Well (Watts, 2012)
Facts at Your Fingertips: Ancient Rome edited by Anita Croy (Wayland, 2009)
Food and Celebrations: Italy by Sylvia Goulding (Wayland, 2008)

Web

http://news.bbc.co.uk/1/hi/world/europe/country_profiles/1065345.stm
Background information, current news and a timeline of major events in Italian history
http://www.kidskonnect.com/component/content/article/26-countriesplaces/318-italy.html
Information about Italy, including links to other websites

Index